IT'S OK TO FEEL SH*T

SOMETIMES

KIND WORDS AND PRACTICAL ADVICE
FOR WHEN YOU'RE FEELING LOW

SAM COOPER

IT'S OK TO FEEL SH*T (SOMETIMES)

Text by Claire Chamberlain

An Hachette UK Company
www.hachette.co.uk

Vie Books, an imprint of Summersdale Publishers Ltd
Part of Octopus Publishing Group Limited
Carmelite House
50 Victoria Embankment
LONDON
EC4Y 0DZ
UK

www.summersdale.com

Printed and bound in China

ISBN: 978-1-80007-703-4

Substantial discounts on bulk quantities of Summersdale books are available to corporations, professional associations and other organizations. For details contact general enquiries: telephone: +44 (0) 1243 771107 or email: enquiries@summersdale.com.

Disclaimer:
This book is not intended as a substitute for the medical advice of a doctor or physician. If you are experiencing problems with your health, it is always best to follow the advice of a medical professional.

CONTENTS

Introduction

If you ever find yourself feeling a bit... well... *sh*t*, welcome to the club. While it can be an uncomfortable – even distressing – feeling, it's also inevitable: your emotions can fluctuate depending on your mental health, resilience, circumstances, hormones and current peer support, so you might feel elated one week and anxious the next. However, if those negative emotions seem to be on the increase, muscling out all the joy in your life, you may need a little support to help you get back to a place where things (hopefully) feel considerably *less* sh*t. So consider this book your very own virtual hug: its pages are filled with practical tips, inspiring ideas and powerful affirmations to help you pick yourself back up when you're feeling low. Ready to unravel those thoughts, feelings and emotions? Let's take a deep dive together...

YOU ARE THE
ONE THING IN THIS
WORLD, ABOVE ALL
OTHER THINGS, THAT
YOU MUST NEVER
GIVE UP ON.

LILI REINHART

WE ALL FEEL SH*T SOMETIMES

LET'S FACE IT, NO ONE'S HAPPY ALL THE TIME.
EVEN THE SHINIEST, SMILIEST PEOPLE EXPERIENCE
DOUBTS, FEARS AND ANXIETY, SO DON'T BE FOOLED:
NOBODY'S LIFE IS PERFECT, HOWEVER IT MAY APPEAR
ON THE OUTSIDE. IF YOU'RE STRUGGLING RIGHT NOW,
SIMPLY KNOWING YOU'RE NOT THE ONLY ONE CAN
HELP YOU FEEL LESS ALONE. THIS CHAPTER EXPLORES
THE WAYS IN WHICH POOR MENTAL HEALTH CAN
AFFECT US ALL. WE REALLY *ARE* IN IT TOGETHER...

WHAT IS MENTAL HEALTH?

Your mental health exists on a spectrum and, as with your physical health, you need to nurture it to keep it ticking along smoothly. Even if your mental health's in great shape, you may still experience difficulties from time to time – anything from a sudden life event (such as a relationship break-up) to a hormonal imbalance will affect it. Sometimes an external event might see you spiralling, while other times you'll be able to take the same triggers in your stride: this is because other changeable factors affect your mental health, including the strength of your support network in that moment and how resilient you feel at any given time.

Living with poor mental health can be lonely, which often exacerbates the situation: feeling low can make it hard to reach out to others at a time when you need their support most. But remember, however isolated you feel, these feelings really do affect most people at some point – the World Health Organization (WHO) estimates one in four people will experience mental health difficulties at some stage. If you're able to open up to someone about how you're feeling, you may be surprised at how much they truly understand.

WHAT MENTAL HEALTH NEEDS IS MORE SUNLIGHT, MORE CANDOUR, MORE UNASHAMED CONVERSATION.

GLENN CLOSE

YES, LIFE'S HARD SOMETIMES... BUT LOOK HOW STRONG YOU ARE

WHAT YOU'RE FEELING IS NORMAL (YES, REALLY)

While feelings of sadness, anxiety and stress can feel hard to handle, they're also perfectly normal. They can sometimes be an appropriate response to a situation you may be living through right now, such as a big life change or bereavement. However, if you're beginning to drift towards feelings of emptiness or "nothingness" for extended periods, or if poor mental health is getting in the way of your daily life, you may be slipping towards a mental illness such as depression. If this is the case, it's important to stop it escalating. There's no shame in asking for help, so consider reaching out to a loved one or asking your doctor for advice.

EMBRACE THE
GLORIOUS MESS
THAT YOU ARE.

ELIZABETH GILBERT

YOU'RE PERFECTLY IMPERFECT

When you're feeling low, do you ever tell yourself you "should" be able to handle it? Or perhaps you start to feel guilty about feeling down, because you think other people have it so much worse than you do? The thing is, going through a difficult time mental health-wise is tough enough, without you berating yourself for it. So take a deep breath (right now) and try to accept yourself, in this very moment, exactly as you are. Allow yourself to feel whatever it is you're feeling, whether that's sadness or anxiety, stress or depression. Understand that even in these low moments, your feelings are valid and you're still wonderful just as you are... difficult emotions and all. Telling yourself otherwise can leave you feeling undeserving of self-love and self-care, which in turn can create unconscious resistance to positive change. This means that, even though you may want things to get better, it's possible to get stuck in a cycle of self-sabotage – for example, constantly telling yourself you don't deserve happiness. Try to accept yourself and be gentle with yourself, because you *do* deserve great things in your life.

YOU'VE GOT THIS!

UNDERSTANDING YOUR MOOD

WHEN THE THUNDER CLOUDS OF A LOW MOOD ROLL IN, THE STORM CAN SOMETIMES KNOCK YOU OFF YOUR FEET. IF THE CAUSE OF YOUR PAIN IS OBVIOUS, SUCH AS A BREAK-UP, YOU MAY HAVE AN IDEA OF HOW TO HANDLE IT, BUT WHEN THE ROOT OF YOUR DISTRESS IS UNCLEAR, YOU CAN BE LEFT FEELING SH*T AND FLOUNDERING AS TO WHY. IN THIS CHAPTER, WE'LL DELVE INTO SOME OF THE CAUSES OF POOR MENTAL HEALTH, TO HOPEFULLY SHED A LITTLE LIGHT ON WHY YOU MIGHT BE FEELING THIS WAY.

THE

BEST TIME

TO PRIORITIZE YOUR MENTAL HEALTH?

RIGHT NOW

WHAT IS LOW MOOD?

Feeling low is common. After all, we all know what it's like to wake up feeling flat: it's not sadness, exactly – you're just not bursting with enthusiasm. The cause of your low mood may be obvious – work pressure or money worries, perhaps. Sometimes there might not be a clear reason why you feel low, but remember, physical issues such as tiredness and dehydration can affect your mood, too. Whatever the cause, it's important to be kind to yourself: eat well, drink plenty of water, take a nap and get some fresh air, as looking after your physical needs will help you to deal with the other things going on in your life.

I FINALLY

REALIZED

THAT OWNING UP TO YOUR

VULNERABILITIES

IS A FORM OF

STRENGTH.

LIZZO

Low mood vs depression

We all feel sh*t sometimes – it's natural. But if the feeling persists it could be a sign of depression. Depression exists on a spectrum: when it's mild, life may feel less worthwhile, but you'll still be able to function. When it's severe, it can make you might question whether life's worth living. Depression is often described as feeling empty or numb – of having no real emotion, either positive or negative. If this is the case for you, it can be hard to tell someone how you're feeling but opening up to a loved one can help. Contact your doctor or a helpline for advice if you think you may have depression.

IS IT MENTAL ILLNESS?

Understanding the distinction between mental health and mental illness is important. Your mental health relates to your emotional and psychological well-being. A mental illness, on the other hand, such as depression or bipolar disorder, may have genetic roots or be linked to brain chemistry.

We all have mental health, and where we are on the mental health spectrum right now depends upon our current circumstances, our ability to be resilient and how supported we feel by those around us. While feeling a bit sh*t can be distressing, we know it will pass and we'll be able to move on (even if this takes time), especially if we practise self-care and go easy on ourselves. Mental illnesses are different, usually requiring professional treatment such as talking therapy or medication, in addition to self-care. Unfortunately, chronic poor mental health can lead to mental illnesses such as depression, so if you're feeling down, commit to addressing it sooner rather than later – it might feel hard at first but it will be worth it in the long run!

NEVER GIVE UP ON YOURSELF

THE TRUTH IS
THAT FALLING HURTS.
THE DARE IS TO KEEP
BEING BRAVE AND FEEL
YOUR WAY BACK UP.

BRENÉ BROWN

STRESS WITH A CAPITAL S

Hands up if you've ever felt stressed? You can place a safe bet that it'll be *everyone*. Exam stress, family stress, work stress, relationship stress – we've all been stressed with a capital S. Stress can actually be *good* sometimes (yes, really) – "positive stress" (known as eustress) is beneficial for motivation and performance. It's only when stress becomes chronic that it can leave you feeling overwhelmed and unable to cope. Stress getting the better of you? It's important to get a handle on it, to stop it manifesting into a mental health problem. The self-care ideas later in this book, such as mindfulness on page 70, should help.

YOU
ARE
GOOD
ENOUGH,
ALWAYS

COPING WITH CHANGE

Big life changes, such as starting university, moving to a new area or leaving a long-term relationship or job, can be scary. While change can often be a good thing, signalling fresh opportunities, that doesn't take away from the fact that it's also challenging. This is because change often goes hand in hand with uncertainty, which by its very nature makes us feel anxious. So, if you're going through a hard time because of an upheaval right now – experiencing nerves, worry or even fear – take a deep breath and recognize those feelings are normal. Sh*t, maybe, but normal.

However, rather than getting paralyzed by these feelings, give yourself credit for doing this big, scary thing. Try this exercise: on a piece of paper, write the words, "Yes, this is scary, but by doing this I'm going to gain..." then list everything you might achieve by diving into change. Next, write: "In a year's time, my life will be/look like..." and jot down a list of all the positive outcomes that could come from this change. Never forget that embracing change takes bravery, and YOU are a badass who can totally do this!

FORGIVE YOUR PAST MISTAKES – WE ALL MAKE THEM

Social media pressure

Yes, social media can be a fantastically creative and inspiring tool, but it's important to recognize the potential it has to damage your sense of self-esteem. When we scroll through other people's online lives – a seemingly never-ending conveyor belt of smiling faces, exotic travel destinations, dream interiors and "perfect" bodies – it has the potential to leave us feeling drab, lonely and, well, *lacking* somehow. If you're beginning to feel social media is becoming a negative force in your life, consider your scrolling habits: how long do you spend on social sites each day? What type of content do you tend to engage with? And – importantly – how does scrolling make you feel, both during and afterwards? Of course, drawing inspiration from others can be fun, but if you end up comparing yourself unfavourably to strangers' homes, bodies or even lives, a screen break might be a good idea. Remember, social media only documents other people's "best bits" – never the ordinary, mundane or negative. No one's life is Instagrammable 24/7 – so yours probably measures up just fine.

HOW TO HANDLE ANXIETY

Anxiety is often characterized by a feeling of worry or dread, usually in relation to a future event (or something you fear might happen). It's common and totally normal, and most people experience it at some point (those butterflies you feel before an exam or presentation? Yep, that's anxiety popping in to say hello). If your anxiety is getting out of hand – for example, if it's constant, your fears are out of proportion to the situation, or you've started avoiding certain situations because of it – it may be a mental health problem. Symptoms are often both mental and physical, and include feeling tense, thinking bad things will happen, dissociation (feeling disconnected from your body), a racing heart, nausea, headaches and shallow breathing. If any of the above resonate with you, it may be worth visiting your doctor. Depending on the symptoms you're experiencing, you might be diagnosed with a specific anxiety disorder, such as generalized anxiety disorder (uncontrollable worry relating to many aspects of everyday life) or social anxiety disorder (fear triggered by social settings) and will then be offered appropriate support. You could also try meditation or yoga classes to help you find positive ways to control your anxiety.

WHAT IS OCD?

If you struggle with obsessive thoughts that lead to repetitive compulsions, you may be suffering with obsessive compulsive disorder (OCD). While these compulsive behaviours (which can include rituals such as hand-washing, checking you've locked the door over again or having to perform a task a certain number of times) may seem to calm the obsessive thoughts, they can take over your life and cause significant stress. OCD can feel scary, but there is help available from trained professionals, so never feel ashamed of opening up to someone close to you or asking your GP for help.

NEVER LET FEAR ROB YOU OF JOY

How to keep calm

A panic attack is an abrupt onset of intense fear that usually lasts anywhere between 5 and 20 minutes. Symptoms often build quickly and can include a racing heart, shallow breath, trembling, sweating and chest pain. While not physically dangerous in itself, a panic attack can be frightening. If you find yourself caught in one, try to focus on breathing as slowly and deeply as you can. Practising deep-belly breathing, regular exercise, eating well to stabilize your blood sugar levels and avoiding caffeine can all help to reduce your stress and anxiety levels, which should make an attack less likely.

LOVING

OTHER

PEOPLE

STARTS WITH LOVING

OURSELVES AND

ACCEPTING

OURSELVES.

ELLIOT PAGE

RAGE (AND HOW TO HANDLE IT)

Let's get something clear: anger is a normal and healthy emotion in the face of frustration, deceit or inequality, although it can also be a sign of depression. When used constructively, it can steer us to respond assertively when we – or those we care about – are mistreated. But if you notice outbursts of rage (verbal or physical) creeping up regularly, it can have pretty negative consequences on every aspect of your life, including your job and your relationships.

When anger strikes, try to give yourself a cooling off "time out" so you can collect your thoughts before you speak or act. A calm response rather than a heated reaction is invariably the best way forward. However, if you're finding that it's too hard to stop the "red mist" clouding your judgement and taking control of your actions, it might be time to seek further support. Check out the Resources section at the back of the book or contact your GP for advice.

WHEN IS IT ADDICTION?

Be honest: have you ever tried to take the edge off a painful, difficult or shameful experience by numbing it with something? The most obvious "something" is alcohol, but in fact, people numb painful experiences with all sort of things: drugs, shopping, sex, work and social media scrolling, to name just a few. The truth is, most of us could probably answer yes to the above. In fact, if you imagine yourself feeling stressed at the end of a busy day, you may also be able to picture yourself reaching for your numbing agent of choice in order to "unwind". The problems start when numbing becomes a habit. As research professor and bestselling author Brené Brown states, "If we numb compulsively and chronically – it's addiction." Addiction is now rightly recognized as a mental illness, but sadly there is still often huge stigma attached to it, so admitting you need help can be difficult. However, support is often crucial to beating addiction, so if you're concerned about your own (or someone else's) numbing habits, don't be shy about asking for help. Your doctor will be able to offer confidential advice about the best first steps to take.

WHAT IS SELF-HARM?

Self-harm (hurting yourself by cutting, scratching or bruising, among others) is a coping mechanism – a way of relieving tension, pressure and emotional pain – in the same way that other "numbing" techniques (such as drinking alcohol) do. Self-harm can be upsetting, is often dangerous and, as with other compulsive or addictive behaviours, it doesn't address the underlying emotional issues. Dealing with these internal issues and learning how to cope without hurting yourself is vital to move beyond self-harm. If you're concerned about yourself (or someone else) you can contact your doctor for confidential advice and support.

I'VE BEEN SEARCHING FOR WAYS TO HEAL MYSELF, AND I'VE FOUND THAT KINDNESS IS THE BEST WAY.

LADY GAGA

DISORDERED EATING

Disordered eating and eating disorders are complex mental illnesses, with many contributing factors as to why a person may struggle with them – and the desire to be thin isn't always the cause. Eating disorders refer to illnesses that can be diagnosed with a specific set of criteria, such as anorexia nervosa, bulimia and binge eating disorder. Disordered eating refers to problems with food that fall outside of these criteria (symptoms might include chronic weight fluctuations or rigid rules about food). Sadly, eating disorders tend to go hand in hand with shame and secrecy, but getting help is important – sometimes lifesaving. You can find information about eating disorder support in the Resources section of this book. Remember, you don't have to go through this sh*t alone, however lonely it feels.

YOU ARE

WORTHY

OF

LOVE

AND

KINDNESS

Fear of failure

In order to lead a fulfilling and rich life, it's important to be brave and go after the opportunities that matter to you, right? But what if fear of failure prevents you from even trying in the first place? First of all, don't berate yourself: fear of failure is common, and when it's chronic, it even has its own name – atychiphobia. Fear of failure often goes hand in hand with perfectionism: after all, if you set yourself high (sometimes unrealistic) standards, nagging worries about failure can become standard. If worries about failure are stopping you living your best life, it may be time to reframe failure. Rather than viewing it as something that should be avoided – perhaps because deep down you believe that failure is a sign you're not good enough (untrue, by the way) – learn to embrace failure. Of course, failing hurts, but it's also a sign you've been brave and tried. What's more, failure isn't a full stop; rather, it's a jumping off point. What can you learn from this experience? Arianna Huffington has said, "Failure is not the opposite of success. It is part of success." So let's all get out there, fail more and live more.

Coping with rejection

It doesn't matter how much you dress it up, rejection hurts. Whether it's from a partner, friendship group, college/job application or anything else, rejection feels like a low blow and can knock everything from your confidence to your self-worth. However, rejection is a part of the human experience (however sh*t it may feel), so learning to cope with it (and even thrive after it happens) is key. Firstly, though, it's important to allow yourself space to grieve the lost opportunity/partnership. Of course it hurts: it mattered to you. Pretending that it didn't isn't going to get you anywhere. If you can allow yourself to lean into that pain, you may find some release in really feeling those difficult feelings. Leaning into pain is not an excuse to start berating yourself, though: this is the time to practise self-kindness, not self-judgement. Treat yourself the way you would a friend who is hurting: compassion is an important step, so don't blame yourself. Once you've begun to process the pain, you can start to work on building your resilience. Focus on how you can grow from the experience and, importantly, stay open to future experiences.

HAVING COMPASSION
STARTS AND ENDS WITH
HAVING COMPASSION
FOR ALL THOSE
UNWANTED PARTS
OF OURSELVES.

PEMA CHÖDRÖN

SPEAK
KINDLY
TO
YOURSELF

Feeling lonely?

There's no doubt about it, loneliness can feel pretty damn sh*t. Whether you're physically spending lots of time alone or you don't feel like you've quite found your tribe yet, loneliness isn't pleasant. But here's something to remember: feeling lonely does NOT mean there is anything wrong with you. Spending time nurturing some close human connections can help to both ease your sense of isolation and build your confidence. Try to think of one person you could call, message or meet up with. Why not join a local art class or sign up to volunteer with a local charity? There's no better time to reach out than the present!

HOPE
SHINES

BRIGHTEST

IN THE

**DARKEST OF
MOMENTS**

I HAVE MET MYSELF
AND I AM GOING
TO CARE FOR
HER FIERCELY.

GLENNON DOYLE

SELF-CARE ISN'T SELFISH

IF YOU HAVE A TENDENCY TO EQUATE SELF-CARE WITH SELF-INDULGENCE, IT MIGHT BE TIME TO CONSIDER A DIFFERENT PERSPECTIVE. FAR FROM BEING SELFISH, SELF-CARE IS ACTUALLY ESSENTIAL MAINTENANCE — AND WE SHOULD ALL BE DOING MORE OF IT IN ORDER TO STAY HEALTHY, HAPPY AND CONTENT. THIS CHAPTER EXPLAINS WHY SELF-CARE CAN BE SO VITAL IN THE FIGHT AGAINST FEELING SH*T, AS WELL AS GIVING YOU SOME TOP SELF-CARE TIPS TO SET YOU ON YOUR WAY.

What is self-care?

Self-care refers to any deliberate and conscious act you undertake that protects and improves your own physical, mental and emotional health. Of course, pampering counts (spa day, anyone?) but it's so much more than that. From eating healthily and daily movement, to mindfulness, meditation and anything that sparks joy for you, self-care can help to relieve stress while nourishing your soul.

IT'S NOT SELFISH TO
LOVE YOURSELF, TAKE
CARE OF YOURSELF,
AND TO MAKE YOUR
HAPPINESS A PRIORITY.
IT'S NECESSARY.

MANDY HALE

All your feelings are valid

Before we delve any further into the realm of self-care, we need to get something straight: practising self-care absolutely does NOT mean denying upsetting or uncomfortable feelings. It's not about stepping into a bubble bath, plastering a smile on your face and telling yourself that everything's perfect when, deep down, you feel terrible. Because the fact is, sometimes sad and scary things happen, and when they do it's normal to feel unhappy and fearful. It's important to recognize these feelings are completely valid.

Self-care isn't a quick fix or cure-all, and you certainly haven't "failed" if practising self-care doesn't make you feel instantly better. However, when you're in this sad, scary place, it's important to be kind to yourself: to think, yes, this is hard and difficult, and maybe I'd rather not be going through it, but it's not my fault, I still matter and I still deserve love and care. In short, self-care is about nurturing yourself – through both the good times and the sh*t times.

Self-care vs damage control

Probably far too many of us are guilty of turning to self-care as a last resort, once our mental health has already taken a nosedive and we're wading knee-deep through those crappy feelings. In this way, it becomes less self-care and more damage control. But it's far harder to navigate those difficult emotions when you're already in the middle of them. Putting self-care practices in place *before* a crisis is more useful. Vowing to make self-care a daily habit is one of the most nurturing, life-affirming things you can do for yourself.

IT'S TIME TO SHOWER YOURSELF WITH LOVE AND KINDNESS

SELF-CARE IS NECESSARY

Still need convincing that self-care is worth it? Then try this for size: research has shown that practising regular self-care can help you become more attuned to your body and needs; reduces stress and anxiety; improves your mental health; and boosts self-esteem. And if that's not enough to get you interested, it can also improve your relationships, which makes sense: if you're stressed and run-down, you have less to give others. Conversely, taking time out for yourself will leave you with more energy and more joy to share with those around you.

SELF-CARE
IS NOT SELFISH.
YOU CANNOT
SERVE FROM AN
EMPTY VESSEL.

ELEANOR BROWN

MAKE TIME FOR SELF-CARE

What with work, studies, commuting, caring responsibilities and chores filling up our already jam-packed schedules, it's no wonder many of us feel we simply don't have time for self-care. But it's so important not to demote yourself to the bottom of your own to-do list (you matter, remember). Scheduling time for self-care, by physically writing it down in your diary or setting an online reminder, means you'll be more likely to follow through with your intention of caring for yourself. It doesn't have to take up much time – some days, it might simply be five minutes of sitting quietly and focusing on your breathing. If time is tight, make use of "fringe" hours – those periods of time, such as early mornings or lunch breaks, that are often underused. Think also about times where you're simply waiting – for a train, for food to cook, for your child's after-school activity to finish. These are perfect moments for self-care. It's time to claim those marginalized minutes for yourself. Everyone has time for self-care, you just need to get in the habit of making it happen!

And breathe...

Ever noticed that when you're stressed or anxious, your breathing becomes more shallow and rapid? Simply performing regular deep breathing techniques can help you feel calmer and can even improve your mood (it's not just anecdotal: science has proven it to be true). For a few minutes each day (or as often as you remember), try slowing and controlling your breath, inhaling for a count of five, then exhaling for a count of five, both through your nose. It has many benefits, from slowing your heart rate and reducing blood pressure, to lowering cortisol levels (the stress hormone).

IT'S TIME TO

CULTIVATE

A SENSE OF

CALM

LIVE MORE MINDFULLY

Mindfulness is more than just a buzzword: practise it daily, and it can help with stress, anxiety and even depression. Mindfulness works by drawing you away from those difficult thoughts and feelings. Being mindful simply means becoming consciously aware of the present moment exactly as it is, without judgement and without trying to change anything. It's a way of reconnecting with the "right now" of life and can be especially helpful in nipping those negative thoughts in the bud. Drawing your attention to the present moment sounds simple but it can take practice, especially if you're used to being stuck in your head along with all those worries and fears, so don't be hard on yourself if you struggle at first. Start with just five minutes, drawing your attention away from your thoughts and out into the world around you. Focus on each sense in turn: what can you see, hear, smell, feel, even taste? If a thought pops into your head that takes your mind away from the present moment, acknowledge it without judgement, then draw your attention back to the present moment. In time, mindfulness can help you become comfortable during times when life feels sh*t.

EMBRACE THIS MOMENT, EXACTLY AS IT IS

WE NEED TO

DO A
BETTER JOB

OF PUTTING OURSELVES

HIGHER ON
OUR OWN

"TO DO" LIST.

MICHELLE OBAMA

THE BENEFITS OF MASSAGE

Hopefully you'll have realized by now that you don't need an excuse to pamper yourself, but if you wanted a scientific reason to push it even higher up your list, here it is: massage offers numerous health benefits, including improved circulation and reduced stress and anxiety symptoms. This makes it a great addition to your self-care arsenal. Book a session with a reputable therapist, ask a partner or friend for a stress-busting shoulder massage, or try this simple self-massage technique: making small circles with your fingertips, massage your scalp using medium pressure for a few minutes, then finish by gently massaging your ear lobes between your thumb and forefinger. Bliss!

PUT
YOURSELF
FIRST
SOMETIMES

SELF-CARE
MEANS GIVING
YOURSELF
PERMISSION
TO PAUSE.

CECILIA TRAN

Try an alternative therapy

While the jury's out as to whether alternative therapies – including aromatherapy, reiki and reflexology – offer benefits in their own right, there's anecdotal evidence to suggest they help to relieve stress and anxiety. And anything that relaxes you has to be a good thing. The alternative therapies mentioned above all aim to improve your physical and mental well-being, as well as aiding relaxation. But keep in mind that alternative therapies aren't a replacement for professional support when it comes to depression and severe anxiety. Speak to your doctor about more traditional support such as talking therapies and medication, alongside anything alternative.

Try meditation

If you think you don't have time to meditate, it's a sign that you'd probably benefit from it! While we all lead full-on lives, taking just five or ten minutes each day to sit quietly in meditation can do wonders for your well-being. Research backs this up: studies show that a regular meditation practice can result in reduced stress and enhanced self-awareness, leaving you in a better place to manage everything life throws at you.

At its core, meditation is simply focused attention. To start, ensure you're in a quiet place and sit comfortably. There are many different ways to meditate, but one of the most common is to simply focus on your breath. Gently close your eyes and follow each inhale and exhale, without trying to change your breathing pattern or force yourself to breathe more deeply than normal. You may find your mind wanders as thoughts arise in your head. This is normal: as soon as you notice your attention has shifted, simply acknowledge the thought, then draw your attention back to your breath. If you'd like support, guided meditations are a great entry point – you can find them online or via a meditation app.

Healthy body, healthy mind

Let's get something straight: this isn't about how you look. It isn't about slimming down or sculpting a physique a bodybuilder would be proud of. Bodies come in all shapes and sizes, and are all capable of different things, and this diversity is something to be celebrated. This is simply about recognizing the fact that looking after your physical health will have a positive knock-on effect for your mind, too. The following tips will give you a few ideas of how to take care of your physical (and therefore mental) health.

BE HEALTHY AND

TAKE CARE
OF YOURSELF

BUT BE HAPPY WITH THE
BEAUTIFUL THINGS

THAT MAKE
YOU, YOU.

BEYONCÉ

YOU ARE AMAZING, EXACTLY AS YOU ARE

MOVE MORE

Exercise is a great way to improve both your physical health and your mental health. It's proven to help reduce stress, and boost feelings of confidence, resilience, self-esteem and happiness. How? By flooding your body with endorphins (the feel-good hormone)! Simply committing to moving more throughout the day is a brilliant way to sneak more exercise into your routine: take the stairs instead of the elevator, walk instead of drive, dance around the kitchen while you wait for the kettle to boil, perform squats while you brush your teeth – anything that gets your heart racing!

You are
what you eat

Eating for happiness is not about restrictive eating or dieting. It's about fuelling yourself with foods that make you feel great! Some of the best brain-boosting foods include those rich in GABA (an amino acid that helps to regulate mood, found in broccoli, brown rice, lentils, bananas, oats and spinach), which has been shown to ease anxiety; and those high in B vitamins (such as leafy greens, salmon and eggs), which can help improve mental health. And of course, all the usual antioxidant-rich fruits and veggies, alongside adequate protein, carbs and healthy fats (such as avocado and oily fish).

NOURISH YOUR MIND, BODY AND SOUL TODAY

I HAVE COME TO
BELIEVE THAT CARING
FOR MYSELF IS NOT
SELF-INDULGENT.
CARING FOR MYSELF
IS AN ACT OF
SURVIVAL.

AUDRE LORDE

STAY HYDRATED

Drinking water is a vital component of protecting your physical health... but did you know it can boost your mood, too? Drinking enough water will help you stay mentally focused, boost concentration levels and mood, and can even help stave off anxiety and fatigue. So, if you're feeling low, something as simple as drinking a glass of water might help, and it certainly won't do any harm! It's recommended that you drink between six and eight glasses a day. Try adding lemon wedges or cucumber slices for flavour, and remember, juices, herbal teas, soups, and even tea and coffee all count.

Limit your alcohol intake

If you've been feeling a bit sh*t recently and you drink alcohol, it's worth considering the fact that, despite the feelings of relaxation that first glass can induce, alcohol is a depressant. Of course, enjoying the odd glass or two isn't a sign of anything untoward, but if you drink often or in large quantities, it's going to have some negative effects on both your mind and body, including heightened anxiety (especially when hungover), disrupted sleep patterns and fatigue. Longer-term effects include liver problems and increased risk of some cancers. It's also worth remembering that alcohol is addictive: if you recognize that you use alcohol as a coping mechanism to numb painful or difficult emotions, it's a sign it could be a problem. It's important to be honest with yourself about your relationship with alcohol. Do you need to cut back? We'd all benefit from sticking to the weekly recommendation of 14 units of alcohol (roughly six medium glasses of wine) or less, with at least two consecutive alcohol-free days a week – and if you've been feeling down, it might be worth steering clear for a while.

ENJOY AN AFTERNOON NAP

Ah, the joys of a midday snooze! What better way to recharge than to snuggle under a blanket and enjoy 20 minutes of shut-eye? Research shows that, as well as reducing sleepiness, a nap can boost concentration and memory recall, as well as improving alertness, so squeezing in a short siesta is something of a win-win, hopefully leaving you feeling more productive later in the day. Try not to nap after 4 p.m., as this could disrupt your night-time sleep, and use an eye mask to block out natural daylight if you struggle to drop off.

ALMOST EVERYTHING
WILL WORK AGAIN
IF YOU UNPLUG IT
FOR A FEW MINUTES,
INCLUDING YOU.

ANNE LAMOTT

SOMETIMES RESTING

IS THE MOST PRODUCTIVE

THING YOU CAN DO

Try a social media detox

It's true that social media is a way of staying connected, but have you ever stopped to consider how this constant connectivity is affecting your mental health? If you're beginning to feel overwhelmed by social media, find yourself getting frustrated by others' posts, feel pressured to constantly post content, or feel caught up in a comparison cycle, a break may be well overdue. Studies show that a detox – anything from a few days to a few months – can help reduce anxiety, improve sleep patterns, boost mental well-being and lessen stress. Is it time to press "pause" instead of "post" for a while?

Mind your mantras

Many people are sceptical about affirmations, without realizing they probably already use them to great effect each day. If you've ever told yourself, "I'm so stressed" or "I'm not good enough" on repeat – and you've started to believe this – that's affirmation in action. Isn't it funny how we're often willing to believe the negative things we tell ourselves, yet find it hard to believe the positive? It's time to replace those negative mantras with some positive ones! "I am enough" or "I'm filled with positive energy" are great examples, or you can choose your favourites from this book. Keep your affirmations short, as this will help you remember them.

YOU ADD SOMETHING WONDERFUL TO THE WORLD

LOVE YOURSELF, CHERISH YOUR QUALITIES AND MARVEL AT YOUR UNIQUENESS.

KATIE PIPER

Lose yourself in a book

Who doesn't love losing themselves in the pages of a good book whenever life gets a bit sh*t? Reading is absorbing, comforting and anxiety-relieving. Research has found that getting lost in a good book can actually lower stress levels, due to the fact that getting caught up in an absorbing storyline allows you to shut out real life for a little while. Escapism at its very best!

HAVE A DUVET DAY

Sometimes, you might feel strong enough to battle on through a difficult day, despite the fact you feel sh*t on the inside. Sometimes, you might be able to smile through it and get stuff done. Other days, you might not. On these days, when your mental health is in a bad place and you're feeling low, it's OK to allow yourself a duvet day: sleep, rest, read, binge on Netflix... whatever it is you feel you need to recuperate and recharge. Tomorrow is another day. So for now, banish the guilt and give yourself permission to rest.

THE REAL
MEDITATION
PRACTICE IS HOW
WE LIVE OUR LIVES
FROM MOMENT
TO MOMENT
TO MOMENT.

JON KABAT-ZINN

Embrace the great outdoors

Spending time outside, soaking up all nature has to offer, comes with a host of well-documented mental health benefits. In fact, many studies have been conducted into the benefits of spending time in nature, with results showing that it can do anything from boosting mood, reducing stress and easing anxiety, to helping alleviate depression.

The Japanese tradition of *shinrin-yoku* (forest bathing) is now being widely adopted by Western cultures, as we start looking to the natural world to improve our mental health. The practice simply involves immersing yourself in nature, by walking slowly through (or sitting quietly in) an area of natural beauty and experiencing it with all of your senses. A forest or woodland setting is perfect, but any natural space, such as a meadow, seashore or even parkland will do your mind the world of good. If you're short of time, even sitting outside with your feet in the grass for five minutes can help you feel more peaceful and reconnected. If this isn't possible, invest in some houseplants to bring a little of the outside into your living space. The goal is to simply appreciate nature's beauty – you might be amazed at how calming yet rejuvenating it can be.

TAKE A COLD-WATER DIP

It might sound unpleasant, but immersing yourself in cold water – either outside in nature or by taking a short cold shower – is an amazing way to get an instant mood boost. A growing tribe of cold-water enthusiasts are extolling the virtues of ice baths, cold showers and wild swimming in the sea, rivers and lakes, due to the numerous purported health benefits. These include boosted immunity, improved circulation and improved mood, due to those feel-good endorphins again. If you're going to get your feel-good cold kicks outdoors by swimming in the wild, safety is paramount. Make sure you are fully prepared and always follow safety guidelines, including using a tow float and never swimming alone (for more information, visit www.rnli.org). You don't need to leap into the ocean to reap the benefits though – simply turning the temperature to cool for 30 seconds at the end of your shower can give you the same glow. Be mindful of health conditions, especially relating to the heart – always consult your doctor if you have concerns.

Time for tea

If the tension drops from your shoulders at the thought of a soothing cup of tea, there's good reason. People have relaxed over cups of tea for thousands of years. In the 1100s, Zen Buddhist tea-drinking ceremonies were created with the aim of aiding meditation. Research shows tea drinking has similar effects on the brain as meditating, as it stimulates alpha brainwaves associated with deep relaxation and enhanced clarity. Bored of regular tea? Simply pick a different variety: peppermint can boost mood and aid digestion, while turmeric, with its antioxidant and anti-inflammatory properties, can improve immune function.

A LITTLE SELF-CARE GOES A LONG WAY

Sleep well

It's official: sleep deprivation is bad for you. Studies show that regular poor sleep can result in impaired memory and flattened emotional responses – so if you're struggling to get quality shut-eye, no wonder you feel sh*t sometimes. Adults need roughly eight hours of sleep each night, although you may need to spend longer in bed to achieve this – perhaps nine hours. Struggling to drop off? Try to maintain a room temperature of 16–8°C; ensure it's dark (a blackout blind can help); and aim to keep noise to a minimum – earplugs can be a lifesaver in noisy urban environments.

LOVE YOURSELF FIRST,
AND EVERYTHING
ELSE FALLS INTO LINE.

LUCILLE BALL

ASKING
FOR HELP

OPENING UP ABOUT YOUR MENTAL HEALTH IS
IMPORTANT IF YOU'VE BEEN STRUGGLING. TELLING
SOMEONE YOU TRUST CAN HELP, AS IT LIFTS THE
BURDEN OF HAVING TO HIDE HOW YOU'VE REALLY
BEEN FEELING AND IS THE FIRST STEP TO BUILDING A
SUPPORT NETWORK. BUT THERE'S NO DENYING THAT
TALKING TO OTHERS ABOUT YOUR MENTAL HEALTH
CAN BE DAUNTING. THIS CHAPTER EXPLORES HOW TO
START THE CONVERSATION, AS WELL AS WHERE TO
FIND SUPPORT IF YOU'D RATHER STAY ANONYMOUS.

You have nothing to be ashamed of

First things first: if you've been bottling up your feelings for a long time, opening up to someone can seem like a huge deal. But remember, you have nothing to be ashamed of. One in four people experience mental health difficulties in developed countries, so you're by no means alone. Struggling to open up? Then put yourself in your loved one's shoes: how would you feel if they opened up to you? Would you secretly brand them as weak? Of course you wouldn't. You'd feel in awe of their bravery and strength. This is the same: there's no shame in asking for help. Ever.

ASKING FOR HELP TAKES COURAGE –

BUT YOU ARE BRAVE

YOU ARE NOT A BURDEN

Are you worried about opening up about your mental health because you feel guilty about burdening another person with your problems? This is a common concern, but it's important to drop it immediately – because it's simply not true. Opening up to someone does not make you a burden, even if your mental health is making you feel that way right now. Remember, the people who care about you will want to be there for you. It's time to let them in.

"POSITIVE VIBES ONLY" ISN'T A THING. HUMANS HAVE A WIDE RANGE OF EMOTIONS AND THAT'S OK.

MOLLY BAHR

ENJOY THE

SUNSHINE,

ACCEPT THE

CLOUDS

HOW TO OPEN UP

If you think confiding in a loved one means sitting opposite them, looking them in the eye and blurting out that you've been feeling utterly sh*t of late, it's no wonder you might be reticent. While this is a great way to open up if you're feeling confident, it's not the *only* way. If you're up for an in-person chat but don't fancy feeling quite so in the spotlight, going for a walk or a drive together can be easier, as you don't need to make intense eye contact if you're side by side. A phone call is good if you'd like a two-way chat but being face to face feels too confrontational. Arrange a time beforehand, so you know they'll be available, and jot down notes so you don't forget anything important.

Writing an email or letter can be therapeutic, as you can craft what you want to say, and you have the silence to explain how you've been feeling and also what support you think you might need. Or if this feels too formal, chatting via SMS or DMs is a great option, and gives you the chance to include links to information.

OPEN UP TO JUST ONE PERSON

There are of course no rules when it comes to telling people about your mental health. However, starting by telling just one person can be less overwhelming than opting for a group setting. Choosing one person you trust, rather than a group of people, also means you'll be more likely to be listened to (and actually heard). Try to ensure you're not going to be interrupted as the person you tell will likely want to be able to give you their full attention, and you're bound to feel calmer knowing no one else is about to burst in or overhear. Inviting a friend or loved one over for a coffee (when you know your house will be otherwise empty) can be a good plan.

Keep alcohol out of it

It's not unusual to try taking the edge off a stressful situation, such as telling someone you're struggling with your mental health, with a glass of wine or two. But before you grab that bottle, try to remember that keeping a clear head while you try to explain what you're going through will make things easier in the long run. Not only is drinking a depressant which will make you feel worse overall, it might also make you forget important details and will likely make you feel more emotional in the moment.

Your loved one's reaction

It's impossible to predict how someone will react when you speak up about a mental health problem, but this shouldn't stop you opening up. The most likely reaction will be concern, love and support. Your loved one might express a sense of relief that you've opened up, especially if they've been worrying about you but haven't known how to talk to you about it. Be prepared for questions – after all, what you're going through isn't new for you, but it might be new to them. Of course, there's a chance they might get upset – it can be hard for people to hear that someone they care about has been suffering. Remember, if they react negatively for whatever reason, it's absolutely not a reflection on you. You're doing a brave and important thing by telling them.

THERE ARE MANY WAYS
OF GETTING STRONG.
SOMETIMES TALKING
IS THE BEST WAY.

ANDRE AGASSI

BAD
MOMENTS
DO PASS

Maintain the conversation

After your initial conversation, try to ensure it doesn't simply end there. Try telling your loved one what support you think you might need from them, so that they know how to move forward in a supportive role that doesn't feel awkward for either of you. Perhaps you might like them to call or message you a few times a week, or maybe you could agree another catch-up soon. If you've told someone about your struggles over the phone or email, getting an in-person catch-up arranged will not only be easier now, but it will probably also be cathartic: being able to chat, hug and laugh together can help to release stress. Your loved one could help in practical terms such as coming out for a run or walk with you if your goal is to exercise more, or maybe even accompanying you to a doctor's appointment if you feel you'd like some extra support.

YOUR SUPPORT NETWORK

It can be super scary telling someone that you're struggling, but once you take this huge step you'll start to grow a support network all around you. One of the great things about telling someone what you've been going through is that you'll have someone on your side who will be able to check in on you when you're feeling low. You could stay as a team of two, or this could simply be the foundations for a wider network, depending on how many people you'd like to tell or how much additional support you need. So be brave and take that difficult first step – you won't regret it!

EVEN THE
STRONGEST
PEOPLE NEED
SUPPORT
NOW AND
THEN

What if you don't want loved ones to know?

Opening up to someone you know can be ideal if you have someone close to you that you trust. But what if no one in your network really fits the bill? Or if you want support, but also want to stay anonymous? The great news is there are so many ways you can find help without having to tell someone who knows you. Remember, wishing to remain anonymous is completely valid: this is your journey, so you get to do it your way.

JUST BECAUSE

NO ONE ELSE

CAN HEAL OR DO YOUR

INNER WORK
FOR YOU

DOESN'T MEAN YOU CAN,
SHOULD, OR NEED TO

DO IT ALONE.

LISA OLIVERA

YOU HAVE
IT IN YOU
TO BE
HAPPY,
CALM AND
CONTENT

Look online for support

There is a wealth of information, advice and support online. This includes mental health websites and online forums, where you can anonymously chat with others. When looking for online support, stay mindful of the source of the information you're accessing. Opt for reputable sites only, such as registered charities or check out the Resources section at the back of this book. Responsible sites will always contain trigger warnings, to keep you safe if you're feeling vulnerable. Self-care apps can offer valuable support too: there are apps for mindfulness, meditation, yoga... even apps that remind you to drink more water, which can be useful when you're feeling sh*t and are less likely to instinctively care for yourself.

YOU CAN LIVE
WELL WITH A
MENTAL HEALTH
CONDITION, AS
LONG AS YOU OPEN
UP TO SOMEBODY
ABOUT IT.

DEMI LOVATO

FEELING SH*T IS NOT A PERMANENT STATE

ENLIST PEER SUPPORT

If you're looking for some human (rather than online) interaction, but you're still not ready to tell someone you know, you can still find some help. There are so many people out there who know what you're going through, who are willing to offer help, guidance and compassion. It's known as peer support. It involves people with lived experience of a particular condition coming together to offer support and advice to others facing the same (or similar) worries. Peer support differs from more traditional professional support, in that there's no qualified expert offering advice. Instead, everyone's invited to share their experiences and insights for the benefit of others. Peer support is often offered in a group setting and can be accessed via your health professional. You can also find peer support programmes online, or groups may be available within your local community or from student services if you're still in education.

IT MIGHT
NOT BE
EASY,
BUT IT
WILL BE
WORTH IT

ASK FOR HELP,

NOT BECAUSE YOU ARE WEAK,
BUT BECAUSE YOU WANT TO

REMAIN STRONG.

LES BROWN

PICK UP THE PHONE

Helplines are a good option if you'd like to remain anonymous, as they will connect you with a person who will listen impartially, without judgement. This means helplines offer a safe space for you to talk through any worries, concerns or problems. The person who answers your call will be a trained specialist or volunteer. They may ask you questions to help you explore those sh*t feelings in greater depth, but they will never offer advice or opinions, and they won't make any decisions for you.

Helplines tend to be free to call and will be confidential, except in certain safeguarding situations – for example, if the person thinks they need to call an ambulance for you. Many helpline volunteers will listen for as long as you need. This makes them a good option if you're experiencing a crisis and want to talk until the immediacy of any thoughts and feelings have passed.

The impact of opening up

If you've been putting on a brave face and hiding the true depths of those difficult, sh*tty feelings out of shame or guilt, you're absolutely not alone. Mental health problems have been in the dark for too long. But times are changing – and by being brave and opening up about your own mental health, you are becoming part of this new, more open and honest framework. Looking after and being accountable for your own mental health can seem like a drop in the ocean, but the bigger picture is so important: by opening up about your own mental health, you never know who else you will inspire to open up and seek help, too. Because ultimately, the more people who feel able to open up in a safe and non-judgemental environment, the easier it will be for everyone to do so – including future generations. So a huge congratulations to you: you have just become a fantastic role model, whether you realize it or not.

WITH DEPRESSION, ONE OF THE MOST IMPORTANT THINGS YOU COULD REALIZE IS THAT YOU'RE NOT ALONE.

DWAYNE JOHNSON

THE BEST WAY OUT IS ALWAYS THROUGH.

ROBERT FROST

FURTHER SUPPORT

PREVIOUS CHAPTERS HAVE EXPLORED SELF-CARE PRACTICES TO BOOST YOUR MOOD, PLUS HOW TO OPEN UP TO OTHERS. BUT SOMETIMES, THIS MIGHT NOT BE ENOUGH. SEEKING PROFESSIONAL SUPPORT CAN SEEM SCARY AND IT MIGHT FEEL LIKE, IN DOING SO, YOUR MENTAL HEALTH PROBLEMS HAVE DEFEATED YOU. BUT THEY HAVEN'T — NOT BY A LONG SHOT. ASKING FOR HELP DEMONSTRATES STRENGTH, COURAGE, RESILIENCE AND A DESIRE TO LIVE LIFE TO THE FULL AGAIN. YOU CAN DO IT.

ASKING
FOR HELP
IS A
SIGN OF
STRENGTH

When to seek professional support

Accepting that your mental health problem goes deeper than simply "feeling a bit sh*t" can be hard. But sadly, people often leave it longer than they should before seeking professional help, for fear they are not "feeling bad enough". Of course, as we've explored, everyone feels low sometimes. So how are you supposed to know when to seek help? Everyone is different and there's definitely no "one size fits all" approach when it comes to mental health. But to give you an idea, it is worth making an appointment with your doctor to chat about your mental health if you experience any of these:

- Your low mood has continued for three weeks or more.

- Your low mood or anxiety is interfering with your day-to-day life, such as your ability to work or interact with family or friends.

- You're struggling to get out of bed in the mornings; or you think people would be better off if you weren't around.

These difficult feelings might feel like they're going to hang around forever, or that this is simply just "you", but they won't and it's not. Seeking professional support can help you understand and manage these feelings, so don't wait any longer.

FINDING THE HELP YOU NEED

When seeking professional support, where do you begin? Who should you turn to? Often the best starting point is to book an appointment with your doctor. There you'll be able to explain how you're feeling in a safe, confidential environment. To prepare for the appointment, write down everything you want to say – getting it down on paper can help formulate your thoughts and will ensure you don't forget any crucial information. Your doctor may be able to discuss various treatments with you or if they feel your needs are more complex, they may refer you to a specialist.

Seek out specialist help

Once you've spoken with your doctor, they may refer you for further treatment. The most common next step is talking therapy, such as cognitive behavioural therapy (CBT), which has been proven in numerous studies to be effective in the treatment of common mental health problems, such as anxiety or depression. CBT is designed to help you understand and change unhelpful thought and behaviour patterns. You'll need to commit to a series of sessions with a therapist, at the end of which you will hopefully have developed a set of coping strategies to help you navigate potential problem situations in the future.

Medication is also available to help treat mental health problems and may be offered alongside talking therapies. Sadly, there is still stigma attached to taking medicines such as antidepressants, but it's nothing to feel ashamed of. Medication can help to ease the often debilitating symptoms of anxiety and depression, and indeed, it's often essential in the treatment of some severe mental illnesses. Medication is always an option worth exploring with your doctor if you are struggling.

VERY LITTLE IS
NEEDED TO MAKE A
HAPPY LIFE; IT IS ALL
WITHIN YOURSELF,
IN YOUR WAY OF
THINKING.

MARCUS AURELIUS

HEALING IS NEVER INSTANT — BUT GIVE IT TIME

EMERGENCY SUPPORT

If you experience a mental health crisis, you'll need to access emergency support. A mental health crisis could be experiencing suicidal feelings, a panic attack, a manic episode, or if you're worried you might self-harm. In short, it's any time you feel your mental health is at breaking point. Emergency support isn't just about professional help: it's drawing on everyone you know who will help you at a time of crisis. So, who might you contact? Is there a loved one who you know will be there for you when you need them? Ask them if it's OK for you to call them if your mental health deteriorates. Keep the phone numbers of 24-hour helplines to hand: the support these helplines offer during times of crisis can be lifesaving.

If you're in immediate danger – for example, if you have harmed yourself, attempted suicide or are considering doing so – you should get to hospital or call for an ambulance. Call a helpline, contact your local crisis team, or make an emergency appointment with your doctor if you feel you have a little more time to access help. Whatever you do, seek help as soon as you can. You are important and valued, and life won't always feel as sh*t as it might do right now.

THE

FUTURE

IS YOURS TO

WRITE

STAY ALIVE

FOR THE PERSON YOU WILL
BECOME. YOU ARE MORE THAN
A BAD DAY OR YEAR.

YOU ARE
A FUTURE

OF MULTIFARIOUS POSSIBILITY.

MATT HAIG

Conclusion

Everybody feels sh*t sometimes – it's part of the ebb and flow of life. So if you're having one of those days when you'd rather stay hidden under the duvet than get up and face the world, you're not alone. To give yourself a fighting chance of waking up tomorrow feeling a bit better, try a few self-care tips and go easy on yourself: it's okay to do whatever you need to do to look after *you* for a while. However, if those sh*t feelings persist, turning into weeks (or even months), it's time to seek help. And don't feel that you have to go it alone; with the right guidance you will start to feel more like yourself again. So never give up on yourself, because brighter days could be just around the corner.

Resources

Anxiety UK: This charity provides information, support and understanding for those living with anxiety disorders. www.anxiety.org.uk

Beat: This eating disorder charity helps to guide and support those with eating disorders, as well as their loved ones. www.beateatingdisorders.org.uk

CALM: The Campaign Against Living Miserably (CALM) is leading a movement against male suicide. thecalmzone.net

Drinkline: The UK's free and confidential national alcohol helpline. 0300 123 1110 (open weekdays 9 a.m.–8 p.m.; weekends 11 a.m.–4 p.m.)

Mind: This mental health charity offers support and advice to help empower anyone experiencing a mental health problem. www.mind.org.uk

Samaritans: A 24-hour, free, confidential helpline, to support you whatever you're going through. www.samaritans.org; 116 123; jo@samaritans.org / jo@samaritans.ie

SANEline: A national, out-of-hours mental health helpline, offering specialist emotional support, guidance and information. www.sane.org.uk; 0300 304 7000, 4 p.m.–10 p.m.; support@sane.org.uk

Switchboard: A listening and support service for LGBTQIA+ people, via phone, email and instant messaging. switchboard.lgbt. 0300 330 0630 (open 10 a.m. to 10 p.m. every day.)

For readers in the United States:

988 Suicide & Crisis Lifeline: 24/7 free, confidential support for those in distress, and crisis resources for loved ones. www.988lifeline.org; 9-8-8

Anxiety & Depression Association of America: Education, training and research for anxiety, depression and related disorders. www.adaa.org

Freedom From Fear: A national non-profit mental health advocacy organization, helping to positively impact the lives of all those affected by anxiety, depression and related disorders. www.freedomfromfear.org

Mental Health America: Promoting the overall mental health of all Americans. www.mhanational.org

Mental Health Foundation: A non-profit charitable organization specializing in mental health awareness, education, suicide prevention and addiction. www.mentalhealthfoundation.org